Generationology 101

Everything You Didn't Know You Didn't Know About Generations

No Cap, G: A Millennial's Guide to Understanding Themselves and Everyone Else

E. Chronos

Dedication

To the curious minds, the bridge builders, and the time travelers of all ages

May this book be a compass, guiding you through the uncharted territory of generations. May it spark conversations, shatter stereotypes, and ignite a celebration of our shared humanity.

Remember, the future is not written in stone, but woven from the threads of every generation's experiences. Let us learn from each other, embrace our differences, and build a world where every voice is heard and every story valued.

With hope and gratitude,
E. Chronos

CONTENTS

Part 1: Cracking the Code - Defining Generations

Chapter 1: Demystifying Generations: What are they and why do they matter?

So, you've stumbled into this strange land called "Generation Land," where everyone speaks a different language and throws around terms like "Gen Alpha" and "Boomer" like they're handing out candy. Don't worry, fellow traveler, I'm your friendly neighborhood generation decoder. Forget those dusty textbooks – we're ditching the jargon and diving headfirst into the fascinating world of what makes each generation tick (or maybe just twitch, depending on who you ask).

Let's start with the basics: **what even are generations?**

Think of them as giant family reunions, but instead of arguing over Aunt Matilda's casserole recipe, we're squabbling over the best way to use emojis (it's winks, fight me). Each generation is shaped by the unique events, technology, and social shifts they grow up with. Boomers had Woodstock and moon landings, Gen X got grunge and dial-up nightmares, and Gen Z? Well, they've got smartphones glued to their palms and enough existential angst to fuel a nuclear reactor.

But why do these labels matter? Because understanding these differences is like having a secret superpower! You'll be able to:

Decode Grandma's Facebook lingo: "Bless your heart" isn't actually a compliment, and "lit" is not how you describe a cozy fireplace.

Ace that job interview: Knowing what motivates different generations will make you a team player superstar (and avoid awkward generational eye rolls).

Build bridges, not walls: Forget the "kids these days" nonsense. We can learn a lot from each other, from the Boomers' resilience to Gen Z's tech-savvy magic.

So, buckle up, time travelers! We're about to embark on a whirlwind tour through the generations, unearthing their quirks, habits, and hidden awesomeness. We'll laugh, we'll cringe, we'll maybe even shed a tear (looking at you, Millennials and your participation trophy trauma). But most importantly, we'll walk away with a newfound understanding of ourselves and the colorful tapestry of human experience.

This ain't your grandma's history lesson, folks. It's a wild ride through pop culture references, hilarious memes, and enough generational stereotypes to fill a comedy club. So, put down your avocado toast (or your Depends, no judgment), grab your smartphone (or your rotary dial, you cool cats), and get ready to demystify the generations once and for all!

P.S. Don't worry, I won't spoil the ending (who's Gen Alpha gonna become? The robot overlords? The emoji masters? Only time will tell!). But one thing's for sure: this generation-hopping adventure is gonna be epic. Let's do this!

Chapter 2: The Timeline Unveiled: Understanding generation boundaries and key events

When is Gen Z? (1996-2012)!

Ah, Gen Z. The digital natives, the meme masters, the avocado toast connoisseurs. But before we dive into their love of side hustles and questionable fashion choices (sorry, mom jeans, we're still not sold), let's answer the burning question: when exactly did this fascinating bunch grace our planet with their presence?

Mark your calendars, folks, because Gen Z officially landed between **1996 and 2012**. That means the oldest Zoomer is rocking out their late twenties right now, while the youngest are still figuring out how to fold a fitted sheet (bless their hearts).

But wait, there's more! Just like that extra slice of pizza you can't resist (don't judge, we've all been there), Gen Z isn't a monolith. There are early Zoomers who witnessed the rise of social media giants and the fall of dial-up internet (remember that screeching sound? Pure torture). Then there are the late Zoomers who were born into a world pre-loaded with smartphones and mastered the art of the perfect TikTok dance before they could even tie their shoes.

So, while the 1996-2012 timeframe is a good starting point, remember that Gen Z is a spectrum of experiences and perspectives. They're the generation that grew up with the Great Recession as their lullaby and the climate crisis as their reality check. They're the activists, the entrepreneurs, the creators who are redefining success and challenging the status quo, all while cracking dank memes and mastering the art of the side hustle.

So next time you see someone rocking a vintage band tee and dropping fire emojis in your group chat, remember: that's Gen Z. They're here, they're loud, and they're ready to change the world, one perfectly curated Instagram story at a time. Buckle up, world, because these digital natives are just getting started!

P.S. Don't worry, we'll dive deeper into the amazing and sometimes confusing world of Gen Z characteristics in the next chapter. Just be warned, it might involve a lot of avocado toast references and explanations of what "Yeet" actually means (spoiler alert: it's not a yoga pose). Stay tuned!

What years are Gen Alpha? (2010-present)

Ah, Gen Alpha. The toddlers wielding tablets like scepters, the babies born with Alexa as their lullaby, the pint-sized powerhouses who might just hold the key to unlocking the future (or at least mastering the art of the virtual reality dance party). But before we get lost in visions of levitating hoverboards and robot companions, let's answer the burning question: **just what years define this generation of miniature marvels?**

Mark your calendars, future historians, because Gen Alpha officially kicked off in **2010 and is still growing strong**! That means the oldest Alpha kiddos are already hitting their teenage years, mastering the art of the eye roll and proving that sass knows no age limit. As for the younger ones? Well, they're busy conquering playgrounds, learning to walk on two legs (and maybe even code?), and reminding us all that the future is bright, shiny, and probably filled with emojis we haven't even invented yet.

But just like those fancy self-lacing sneakers your nephew keeps begging for, Gen Alpha isn't one-size-fits-all. There's a whole spectrum of experiences within this generation. The early Alphas, born between 2010 and 2014, witnessed the tail end of the analog world and the rise of the smartphone revolution. They're the ones who might understand the thrill of dial-up internet (even if they never actually experienced it themselves!). Then there are the late Alphas, born from 2015 onwards, who are truly digital natives. They navigate augmented reality games like pros, speak the language of TikTok dances, and probably wouldn't even know what to do with a rotary phone (bless their tech-savvy hearts).

So, while the 2010-present timeframe is a good starting point, remember that Gen Alpha is a kaleidoscope of possibilities.

They're the generation that's grown up with climate change as a constant background hum, social media as their second language, and a world where robots are no longer science fiction but a potential next-door neighbor. They're the creators, the innovators, the problem-solvers who might just save the world, one eco-friendly app at a time.

So next time you encounter a tiny human sporting a tablet tan and dropping Minecraft lingo like it's hotcakes, remember: that's Gen Alpha. They're here, they're adorable (even when they're throwing food), and they're ready to redefine the future, one pixelated adventure at a time. Buckle up, world, because these mini masters of the universe are just getting started!

P.S. Don't worry, we'll dive deeper into the fascinating (and sometimes baffling) world of Gen Alpha characteristics in the next chapter. Just be warned, it might involve a lot of virtual reality explanations, discussions about self-driving hoverboards, and deciphering the secret language of emoji combinations. Stay tuned!

When did Gen Z start and end?

Ah, generations. Those nebulous chunks of humanity we neatly box up based on shared experiences and questionable fashion choices. Today, we're putting Gen Z under the microscope, specifically answering the burning question: **when did this internet-savvy, avocado-toast-loving crew first grace our planet**?

Strap yourselves in, time travelers, because we're about to blast off on a journey through the timeline! Buckle up and get ready for some major nostalgia (for some of you, at least).

The Rise of the Zoomers:

The official landing zone for Gen Z is **between 1996 and 2012**. That means the oldest Zoomers are rocking their late twenties right now, probably perfecting their side hustle game while mastering the art of the perfectly curated Instagram story. The younger bunch, meanwhile, are still figuring out how to fold a fitted sheet and navigate the treacherous waters of high school (bless their hearts).

But hold on, fellow history buffs! Just like that extra slice of pizza you can't resist (don't judge, we've all been there), Gen Z isn't one giant pizza pie. There are early Zoomers who witnessed the rise of social media giants and the fall of dial-up internet (remember that ear-splitting screech? Pure torture!). Then there are the late Zoomers who were born into a world pre-loaded with smartphones and mastered the art of the perfect TikTok dance before they could even tie their shoes.

The Shifting Sands of Time:

So, while the 1996-2012 timeframe is a good starting point, remember that Gen Z is a spectrum of experiences and perspectives. They're the generation that grew up with the Great Recession as their lullaby and the climate crisis as their reality check. They're the activists, the entrepreneurs, the creators who are redefining success and challenging the status quo, all while cracking dank memes and mastering the art of the side hustle.

But here's the kicker: even though those 1996-2012 dates are etched in stone (well, not literally, but you get the picture), defining the exact "end" of Gen Z is a bit trickier. Some experts argue that 2012 is a clean cutoff, while others think the Gen Z ship keeps sailing until around 2015. It's all about that sweet spot of shared cultural touchstones and formative experiences.

So, what does it all mean?

Well, understanding these generational boundaries is less about drawing lines in the sand and more about appreciating the unique tapestry of human experience. Each generation comes with its own set of challenges, triumphs, and, yes, questionable fashion choices. By recognizing these differences, we can build bridges, foster understanding, and maybe even learn a thing or two from each other along the way.

Remember, folks, this ain't your grandma's history lesson. This is a wild ride through pop culture references, hilarious memes, and enough generational stereotypes to fill a comedy club. So buckle up, world, because these digital natives are just getting started!

P.S. Don't worry, we'll dive deeper into the amazing and sometimes confusing world of Gen Z characteristics in the next chapter. Just be warned, it might involve a lot of avocado toast references and explanations of what "Yeet" actually means (spoiler alert: it's not a yoga pose). Stay tuned!

Generations by year: A handy reference guide

Ever feel lost in the jungle of generations? Can't tell your Boomers from your Zoomers? Fear not, fellow time travelers! This handy guide is your Rosetta Stone for deciphering the human timeline, one year at a time.

- **1901-1927: The Greatest Generation**: They weathered wars, dust bowls, and economic meltdowns, building resilience like nobody's business. Think stoicism, sacrifice, and a healthy dose of "can-do" spirit.
- **1928-1945: The Silent Generation**: Witnessing the Greatest Generation's heroics, they embraced practicality and hard work. Think quiet strength, conformity, and a knack for getting things done, no fuss, no muss.
- **1946-1964: The Baby Boomers**: They challenged authority, embraced individuality, and, well, boomed the population. Think idealism, rebellion, and a whole lot of bell-bottoms and Woodstock vibes.
- **1965-1980: Generation X**: Latchkey kids and MTV masters, they're the cynical realists who saw the

Boomers' dreams turn dusty. Think independence, resourcefulness, and a healthy dose of "whatever."

- **1981-1996: Millennials**: Raised on technology and optimism, they're the avocado toast-loving, side hustle-hustling, participation trophy generation. Think tech-savvy, ambitious, and maybe a little burned out (but who isn't these days?).
- **1996-2012: Generation Z:** Born with smartphones in their cribs and social media as their lullaby, they're the digital natives redefining everything. Think activism, entrepreneurship, and a side of dank memes and existential angst.
- **2010-Present: Generation Alpha**: The future is here, and it's wearing a VR headset and coding their own breakfast cereal. Think adaptability, inclusivity, and a whole lot of "what's a rotary phone?"

Remember, folks: These are just rough outlines. Each generation is a kaleidoscope of experiences, and the lines get blurry at the edges. But with this handy guide in your pocket, you'll be navigating the generational landscape like a pro, ready to bridge the gap and build a future where avocado toast and vinyl records can coexist in harmony.

Bonus Tip: Want to know exactly where you fall on the spectrum? Check your birth year! And remember, your generation is just one piece of the puzzle. What makes you unique? That's the real treasure!

Now go forth, fellow time travelers, and explore the fascinating world of generations! Just don't forget to bring your sense of humor and a healthy dose of open-mindedness. The future is a wild ride, and we're all in it together!

Chapter 3: Beyond the Labels: Characteristics that define each generation

Unpacking Gen X: Resilience, cynicism, and independence (1965-1980)

Ah, Gen X. The middle child of the generational sandwich, often overshadowed by the booming Boomers and the avocado-toast-wielding Millennials. But don't underestimate these latchkey kids and MTV masters! They're the masters of resilience, cynicism with a wink, and independence that would make MacGyver proud.

Let's crack open the Gen X toolbox and see what makes them tick:

- **Resilience forged in fire**: Growing up with working parents and a healthy dose of "figure it out yourself," Gen Xers learned to be resourceful and adaptable. They're the duct tape and paperclip brigade, the ones who can fix a flat tire with a shoelace and a can of WD-40 (and maybe a sarcastic mutter under their breath).
- **Cynicism with a side of humor**: Witnessing the Boomers' idealism crash and burn, Gen X developed a healthy dose of skepticism. But it's not all doom and gloom! Their cynicism is laced with wit and a dry sense

of humor that could make even the most existential crisis feel like a sitcom.

- **Independence that runs deep**: Raised on a steady diet of self-reliance, Gen Xers value their freedom above all else. They're the DIY champions, the ones who build their own furniture, fix their own cars, and generally prefer to do things their own way, thank you very much.

- **Tech-savvy but not tech-obsessed**: Sure, they grew up with the rise of personal computers and witnessed the internet explode, but Gen Xers aren't glued to their screens. They appreciate the power of technology but also know how to unplug and disconnect, which is a skill we could all learn a thing or two from.

- **Masters of the side hustle**: Before "side hustle" was even a term, Gen Xers were juggling multiple jobs, freelance gigs, and entrepreneurial ventures. They're the jack-of-all-trades, always on the lookout for the next opportunity to make a buck and build their own path.

But remember, folks: Gen X is not a monolith. There are punk rockers and preppies, slackers and go-getters, grunge lovers and yuppies. But one thing unites them: a shared experience of growing up in a world that was changing faster than they could keep up.

So next time you see someone rolling their eyes at the latest TikTok trend or fixing a leaky faucet with a rubber band and a prayer, remember: that's probably a Gen Xer. They're the quiet heroes, the ones who keep the world running with a healthy dose of cynicism, independence, and a whole lot of MacGyver-worthy ingenuity.

P.S. Don't worry, we'll dive deeper into the fascinating world of Gen X music, fashion, and pop culture in the next chapter. Just be warned, it might involve a lot of flannel shirts, cassette tapes, and references to "Smells Like Teen Spirit." Stay tuned!

The Zoomer Generation: Digital natives, activists, and entrepreneurs (1996-2012)

Hold onto your avocado toast, folks, because we're diving headfirst into the world of Gen Z, the digital natives who were born with smartphones glued to their palms and a side of existential angst for breakfast. Buckle up, time travelers, because this generation is like a hyper-caffeinated roller coaster ride of memes, activism, and side hustles that will leave you both exhilarated and slightly confused.

Let's crack open the Zoomer vault and see what treasures we find:

- **Digital Natives**: Born into a world pre-loaded with apps, social media, and the constant hum of the internet, Zoomers are fluent in the language of emojis, memes, and viral trends. They can navigate TikTok dances like pros, master the art of the perfect Instagram story, and probably explain blockchain technology in their sleep.

- **Activism for Breakfast**: Witnessing climate change, social injustice, and political turmoil as their reality check, Zoomers are passionate about making a difference. They're the climate strike champions, the social justice warriors, the ones who organize protests on Twitter and raise awareness with viral hashtags. They're not just talking the talk, they're walking the walk, and they're not afraid to hold anyone, including their own elders, accountable.

- **Entrepreneurial Spirit on Fleek**: Forget lemonade stands, Zoomers are building empires with side hustles before they can even vote. They're the Etsy crafters, the YouTube influencers, the freelance coders who can turn a passion into a paycheck before you can say "dropshipping." They're redefining success, challenging traditional career paths, and proving that hustle and creativity can be the ultimate currency.

- **Mental Health Matters**: While sometimes masked by memes and sarcasm, Zoomers are more open about mental health than any generation before them. They're the ones talking about anxiety on TikTok, destigmatizing therapy with vlogs, and creating safe spaces for open dialogue about mental well-being. They're breaking the silence, challenging the stigma, and reminding us all that it's okay to not be okay.

- **Humor that's Dank and Deep**: Don't let the dank memes and absurd humor fool you, Zoomers are a generation with a sharp wit and a deep understanding of the world. Their humor is a coping mechanism, a way to laugh at the absurdity of life, and a powerful tool for connecting with each other. So, next time you encounter a meme that makes you snort your coffee, remember: there's probably a whole lot of truth hidden behind the humor.

But remember, folks: Gen Z is not a monolith. There are gamers and activists, artists and entrepreneurs, introverts and extroverts. They're a kaleidoscope of experiences and perspectives, all united by their digital native status and a shared desire to make the world a better place, one meme at a time.

So next time you see someone sporting a vintage band tee and cracking fire emojis in your group chat, remember: that's a Zoomer. They're here, they're loud, and they're ready to change the world, one sustainable side hustle at a time. Buckle up, world, because these digital natives are just getting started!

P.S. Don't worry, we'll dive deeper into the fascinating world of Zoomer slang, fashion, and pop culture in the next chapter. Just be warned, it might involve a lot of TikTok explanations, discussions about self-driving hoverboards, and deciphering the secret language of emoji combinations. Stay tuned!

Gen Alpha's Emerging Story: Adaptability, inclusivity, and global awareness (2010-present)

Ah, Gen Alpha. The toddlers wielding tablets like lightsabers, the babies born with Alexa as their lullaby, the tiny humans who might just hold the key to unlocking the future (or at least mastering the art of the virtual reality dance party). But before we get lost in visions of self-driving hoverboards and robot companions, let's crack open the mystery box of their emerging story.

Think of Gen Alpha as a blank canvas, splashed with the vibrant colors of:

- **Adaptability**: They've grown up in a world where change is the only constant. Climate shifts, technological leaps, and shifting social landscapes are their playground. They're the masters of adjusting, the chameleons of the digital age, ready to roll with the punches (or virtual reality punches, as it were).
- **Inclusivity**: Diversity is their norm, not their exception. They see the world through a kaleidoscope of cultures, abilities, and backgrounds. They're the empathy champions, the ones who break down walls and build bridges, reminding us all that "different" is just another word for "awesome."
- **Global Awareness**: The internet is their passport, the world their classroom. They're citizens of a global village, connected to every corner of the planet with a tap of a finger. They understand the interconnectedness of everything, from climate change to social justice, and they're not afraid to use their voice to make a difference, one Instagram story at a time.
- **Technological Savvy**: They don't just speak the language of tech, they practically invented it. Artificial

intelligence, virtual reality, and robotics are their playground. They're the app whisperers, the coding wizards, the ones who might just build the future we can only dream of right now.

- **Boundless Creativity**: Forget coloring inside the lines, Gen Alpha is redefining the lines themselves. They're the artists who code, the musicians who mix beats with AI, the storytellers who craft narratives in virtual worlds. They're pushing the boundaries of creativity, reimagining what art can be, and leaving us all scratching our heads (in a good way) wondering what's next.

But remember, folks: Gen Alpha is still a work in progress. They're the toddlers building sandcastles on the beach of the future, figuring out how to navigate the waves of change and possibility. Their story is just beginning to unfold, and we're all privileged to be witnesses.

So next time you encounter a tiny human sporting a VR headset and dropping AI-generated poetry bombs, remember: that's Gen Alpha. They're here, they're curious, and they're ready to paint the world with their own unique brushstrokes. Buckle up, world, because these mini masters of the unknown are just getting started!

P.S. Don't worry, we'll dive deeper into the fascinating world of Gen Alpha's learning styles, technological playgrounds, and evolving values in the next chapter. Just be warned, it might involve a lot of virtual reality explanations, discussions about robot companions, and deciphering the secret language of emojis Gen Alpha hasn't even invented yet. Stay tuned!

Chapter 4: A Look Back: Exploring the characteristics of Millennials and beyond

The Echo Boomers: Optimism, achievement, and changing expectations (1981-1995)

Ah, the Echo Boomers. Sandwiched between the iconic Boomers and the tech-savvy Millennials, they're often overshadowed, but don't let that fool you. This generation is a powerhouse of optimism, achievement, and a healthy dose of "can-do" spirit. Buckle up, time travelers, because we're diving headfirst into the Echo Boomer world!

Think of them like a well-brewed cup of coffee:

- **Optimism frothed to perfection**: Raised on the tail end of the economic boom and the echoes of their Boomer parents' idealism, Echo Boomers are glass-half-full kind of folks. They believe in hard work, perseverance, and the power of a positive attitude. They're the ones who chase their dreams with a smile and a can-do spirit, even when the world throws them a curveball (or a latte spill, as it were).
- **Achievement brewed strong**: Education is their middle name, and success their favorite flavor. Echo Boomers are driven to excel, whether it's climbing the corporate ladder, mastering a new skill, or becoming the ultimate family champions. They're the ones juggling

demanding careers, raising kids, and still finding time to volunteer and make a difference. Think high achievers with a heart of gold.

- **Changing Expectations – a hint of bittersweet**: While they inherited the Boomer work ethic, their expectations for career and life balance are a tad different. Echo Boomers value flexibility, purpose, and a healthy work-life harmony. They're not afraid to break the mold, pursue unconventional careers, and prioritize their well-being. Think ambitious with a dash of self-care.

- **Tech-savvy with a touch of nostalgia**: They grew up with the rise of the internet but weren't born with a smartphone in their hand. Echo Boomers embrace technology, but they also cherish the analog world. They're the ones who can code their way out of a jam but still appreciate a good vinyl record and a handwritten note. Think digital natives with a vintage soul.

- **A generation bridging the gap**: Echo Boomers are the bridge between the Boomers' optimism and the Millennials' tech-savvy. They understand both sides, acting as translators, mediators, and collaborators. They're the ones who can explain TikTok to their parents and blockchain to their kids, all while building a future that embraces both the old and the new. Think adaptability with a sprinkle of wisdom.

But remember, folks: Echo Boomers are not a monolith. There are artists and entrepreneurs, athletes and scholars, dreamers and pragmatists. They're a diverse bunch united by their shared experiences and a can-do spirit that's hard to match.

So next time you meet someone who's juggling a demanding career, raising a family, and still volunteering at the local soup kitchen with a smile, remember: that's probably an Echo Boomer. They're the quiet achievers, the optimists with a plan, and the generation that's quietly shaping the future, one cup of coffee and well-placed dream at a time.

Remembering the Baby Boomers: Defining individuality and challenging norms (1946-1964)

Ah, the Baby Boomers. The bell-bottom-wearing, Woodstock-rocking, rule-breaking rebels who redefined **"individuality"** and left an indelible mark on the world. Brace yourselves, time travelers, because we're blasting off on a rocket ship fueled by idealism, rock n' roll, and a whole lot of change.

Picture a record skipping over the good parts:

- **Defining Individuality**: Forget cookie-cutter conformity. Boomers were all about carving their own paths, expressing themselves loud and proud. From psychedelic art to anti-war protests, they challenged the status quo and embraced anything but the mainstream. Think flower power meets fist-pumping rebellion.
- **Challenging Norms**: Tradition? Psh, who needs it? Boomers questioned everything from gender roles to

political authority. They fought for civil rights, environmental protection, and the freedom to just, well, be themselves. Think peace signs and sit-ins, all with a healthy dose of rock n' roll attitude.

- **Breaking Barriers**: Shattering glass ceilings is their middle name. Boomers opened doors for women in the workplace, championed diversity and inclusion, and paved the way for future generations to dream bigger and bolder. Think shattering stereotypes and rewriting the rules, all with a touch of groovy confidence.

- **Optimism on Vinyl**: Despite facing wars, economic turbulence, and social upheaval, Boomers held onto a fierce optimism. They believed in the power of progress, the potential of humanity, and the ability to change the world for the better. Think idealism with a can-do spirit, even when the world threw them curveballs (or bad acid trips, as it were).

- **Leaving a Legacy that Rocks**: From music that still makes our ears perk up to advancements in technology and social justice, the Baby Boomer impact is undeniable. They're the ones who gave us Woodstock, fought for LGBTQ+ rights, and questioned everything with a guitar riff and a megaphone. Think game-changers who shook the world and left us with a whole lot of cultural treasures to groove to.

But remember, folks: Boomers are not a monolith. There are hippies and yuppies, rebels and conformists, artists and entrepreneurs. They're a diverse bunch united by their shared experiences and a spirit of change that echoed through the decades.

So next time you see someone sporting a vintage peace sign necklace or belting out a classic rock anthem, remember: that's probably a Baby Boomer. They're the ones who rocked the world, danced to their own tune, and continue to inspire us to challenge the status quo, one protest song at a time.

Ah, the tapestry of human history! Each generation adds a vibrant thread, a unique texture, woven together into the grand story of our ever-evolving world. Today, we're focusing on a crucial section of that tapestry - the Silent Generation and beyond, where stoicism, innovation, and digital natives collide!

First, let's rewind to the stoic heroes:

- **The Silent Generation (1928-1945):** Born amidst the dust storms and shadows of war, they learned resilience like a badge of honor. Think quiet strength, unwavering work ethic, and a "can-do" spirit forged in the fires of hardship. They rebuilt nations, raised families, and laid the foundation for the booming years to come.

Next, we catapult into the era of rebellion:

-

- **Baby Boomers (1946-1964):** The bell-bottomed brigade, the champions of individuality, and the generation that rocked the world to its core. Think flower power, anti-war protests, and a relentless pursuit of social justice. They challenged norms, embraced diversity, and left a legacy of change that still echoes today.

Then, we enter the digital age:

- **Generation X (1965-1980):** Latchkey kids turned tech-savvy masters, they witnessed the rise of the internet and the fall of the Berlin Wall. Think cynicism with a wink, independence that runs deep, and a knack for navigating a world in constant flux. They're the resourceful jacks-of-all-trades, the masters of the side hustle, and the pioneers of a new era.

Now, the baton passes to the tech-natives:

- **Millennials (1981-1996):** Raised on avocado toast and smartphone screens, they're the socially conscious, entrepreneurial champions of the digital age. Think global awareness, boundless creativity, and a relentless pursuit of purpose. They're redefining success, challenging the status quo, and building a future fueled by innovation and inclusivity.

And the future beckons with a new generation:

- **Generation Z (1997-2012):** Born with a tablet in their cradle and activism as their lullaby, they're the masters of adaptability, the champions of mental health awareness, and the digital natives who speak the language of memes and social change. Think inclusivity, entrepreneurship, and a deep understanding of the interconnectedness of the world.

But remember, folks: Each generation is a kaleidoscope of experiences, personalities, and perspectives. These are just broad brushstrokes on a vibrant canvas. The Silent Generation isn't silent anymore, sharing their stories with a new generation eager to learn. Boomers are still rocking, adapting their fight for justice to the digital age. And the younger generations, with their unique blend of experiences, are building a future that's inclusive, innovative, and maybe even a little bit meme-filled.

So, let's celebrate the tapestry of generations, not compare them. Let's learn from the Silent Generation's resilience, embrace the Boomer's spirit of change, appreciate Gen X's resourcefulness, and be inspired by the Millennials' and Gen Z's vision for a better future. Together, we can weave a future that's as diverse and vibrant as the generations who came before us!

Part 2: Navigating the Crossroads - Generations in Dialogue

Chapter 5: Bridging the Gap: Understanding and appreciating generational differences

Gen Z vs. Gen Alpha: Similarities, differences, and the future of communication

Hold onto your fidget spinners, folks, because we're about to dive into a digital duel between two generations that practically speak in emoji: Gen Z and Gen Alpha! These tech-savvy superstars might share the same internet playground, but there's a whole lotta difference between a TikTok dance and a VR coding session. Buckle up, time travelers, as we explore the similarities, differences, and the future of communication in a world where everyone's got a smartphone glued to their palm.

Similarities:

- **Digital Natives**: Forget cave paintings, these generations grew up with screens as their babysitters and algorithms as their friends. They're fluent in meme language, masters of the swipe-and-scroll, and can probably navigate the dark web blindfolded (don't try that at home, kids).
- **Activism on Fleek**: Whether it's climate change or social justice, both Gen Z and Alpha are passionate about making a difference. They're the ones organizing

online protests, spreading awareness with viral hashtags, and holding everyone, from influencers to politicians, accountable.

- **Entrepreneurial Spirit**: Side hustles aren't just a hobby, they're a way of life for these generations. They're the Etsy shop owners, the YouTube vloggers, the freelance coders who can turn a passion into a paycheck before you can say "dropshipping." Think "hustle and flow" with a digital twist.

Differences:

- **Meme Masters**: Gen Z perfected the art of the dank meme, using humor as a coping mechanism and a way to connect with their tribe. Alpha, on the other hand, is all about the meta-meme, the ironic, self-aware humor that breaks the fourth meme wall (whatever that means). Think "memeception" with a side of existential dread (but still funny, somehow).
- **Attention Spans**: Gen Z multitasks like a pro, juggling school, social media, and side hustles all at once. Alpha, on the other hand, operates in hyper-focused bursts, switching between activities faster than a hummingbird on Red Bull. Think "butterfly brain" meets "laser focus" in a digital dance party.
- **The Future of Communication**: Gen Z is all about authenticity and transparency, preferring direct communication over filtered selfies. Alpha, however, is the master of curated online personas, using avatars and virtual worlds to express themselves in ways the real

world just can't. Think "digital doppelgangers" meet "unfiltered realness."

The Future of Communication:

So, what does this all mean for the future of communication? Well, get ready for a wild ride! Imagine a world where memes bridge cultural divides, VR meetings are the new coffee date, and everyone has a personalized digital avatar who can express their wildest dreams (and deepest anxieties). It's a future where Gen Z's authenticity meets Alpha's adaptability, creating a communication landscape as diverse and vibrant as the emojis themselves.

But remember, folks: These are just broad brushstrokes on a digital canvas. Each generation is a unique blend of experiences, personalities, and perspectives. The key is to bridge the wifi gap, to learn each other's languages (meme-speak included), and to build a future where everyone has a voice, regardless of whether they prefer emojis or face-to-face chats.

So, the next time you see a Gen Z'er rocking a vintage band tee and a Gen Alpha kid building a robot in Minecraft, remember: they're not so different after all. They're both just trying to navigate this crazy digital world, one meme, one virtual reality handshake, and one side hustle at a time. And that, my friends, is a future worth connecting with.

P.S. Want to go deeper into the slang, trends, and communication styles of Gen Z and Gen Alpha? Stay tuned, because we're about to crack the code on their digital dialects and unlock a whole new world of understanding!

From Boomers to Alphas: Learning from each other's experiences

Hold onto your avocado toast and dust off your vinyl records, folks, because we're about to embark on a time travel adventure through generations! Today's destination? The fertile ground of intergenerational understanding, where Baby Boomers swap stories with Gen Z over TikTok dances, and Silent Generation stoicism meets Gen Alpha's digital wizardry. Buckle up, time travelers, because the only thing faster than the internet is the wisdom we can glean from each other's experiences!

Think of generations like a delicious family recipe, each adding a unique flavor:

The Silent Generation (1928-1945): The stoic grandparents of the bunch, they weathered wars and economic storms with grit and grace. They'll teach us the value of resilience, hard work, and the quiet power of a well-placed casserole (seriously, their gravy is legendary).

The Baby Boomers (1946-1964): The rule-breaking rockers, the bell-bottomed rebels who challenged the status quo and demanded change. They'll show us the importance of fighting for what we believe in, embracing individuality, and never letting the establishment get away with a bad disco song (seriously, disco wasn't all that bad, Boomers).

Generation X (1965-1980): The latchkey kids turned resourceful masters, they saw the world change faster than a cassette tape rewind. They'll teach us adaptability, independence, and the art of making a mean macrame plant hanger (seriously, macrame is back, Gen Z, thank your Gen X parents).

Millennials (1981-1996): The tech-savvy avocado toast champions, they're redefining success, embracing inclusivity, and fighting for a better planet, one Instagram story at a time. They'll show us the power of social media for good, the importance of mental health awareness, and how to make a killer latte (seriously, Millennials perfected the art of the latte, hands down).

Generation Z (1997-2012): The digital natives who speak meme, the masters of activism and side hustles, they're building the future with VR headsets and a healthy dose of existential angst. They'll teach us the power of humor and self-awareness, the importance of global responsibility, and how to code a robot that can make a decent cup of tea (seriously, Gen Z, teach us your robot tea-making skills).

Generation Alpha (2010-present): The toddlers with tablets as toys and the future CEOs of Mars, they're the blank slate of the bunch, ready to write their own story. They'll remind us of the importance of curiosity, the endless possibilities of technology, and how to build a sandcastle that would make Michelangelo jealous (seriously, Gen Alpha, your sandcastle skills are next-level).

But remember, folks: Generations aren't monoliths. There are artists and entrepreneurs, activists and athletes, dreamers and pragmatists in each and every one. The key is to embrace the differences, learn from each other's strengths, and build bridges instead of walls.

So, the next time you see a Gen Z'er sporting a vintage band tee debating climate change with a Silent Generation veteran over a plate of cookies, remember: that's the magic of intergenerational understanding. It's about sharing wisdom, laughing at memes, and realizing that we're all just travelers on this crazy journey called life.

P.S. This is just the beginning! Craving a closer look at their communication styles and slang? Stay tuned, because we're about to embark on a journey through time, one generation, one avocado toast recipe, and one epic dance party at a time!

Chapter 6: Beyond the Labels: Building bridges and fostering intergenerational understanding

Overcoming stereotypes: Recognizing the individuality within each generation

Ah, generations! Those neatly labeled boxes we try to shove everyone into, with Boomers as rockin' rebels, Millennials as avocado-wielding social media masters, and Gen Z as meme-speaking masters of the side hustle. But hold on, time travelers, because here's the reality: **stereotypes are about as useful as a dial-up connection in the age of fiber optic. They're dusty, inaccurate, and frankly, a bit boring.**

Instead of squinting through stereotype-tinted glasses, let's open our eyes to the kaleidoscope of individuals within each generation! Think of it like a disco party under a rainbow: Boomers with dazzling bell-bottoms dancing alongside Gen Z in VR headsets, Silents quietly crafting wisdom beads next to Alpha kids building robot companions.

Here's why ditching stereotypes is the real dance move:

- **Every generation is a diverse bunch**: Just because someone was born between certain years doesn't mean they all share the same personality, dreams, or love for questionable fashion trends (yes, looking at you, 80s leg warmers).

- **Labels limit our understanding**: When we stick people in boxes, we miss out on the richness and complexity of their experiences. Every individual has a unique story, shaped by their own history, passions, and quirks.

- **Stereotypes create walls, not bridges**: Judging people based on generalizations instead of getting to know them as individuals breeds division and misunderstanding. We're all in this crazy human experience together, let's ditch the labels and build bridges instead!

So, how do we celebrate the individuality within each generation?

- **Start with curiosity**: Instead of assuming you know someone based on their birth year, ask questions, listen to their stories, and discover the amazing person they are.

- **Challenge your own biases**: We all have them, but that doesn't mean we can't work on them. Be mindful of your assumptions and actively seek out diverse perspectives.

- **Celebrate the unique tapestry of humanity**: Every generation, every individual, adds a vibrant thread to the grand story of humankind. Let's appreciate the differences, learn from each other, and dance together under the rainbow of individuality.

Remember, folks: Stereotypes are just boring party guests who nobody really likes. Ditch them, embrace the individuality, and get ready to groove to the rhythm of human diversity! You never know, you might just learn the coolest robot dance move from a Gen Alpha kid or discover a hidden passion for disco from a Silent Generation master. After all, that's the magic of stepping outside the labeled boxes and embracing the full spectrum of who we are. Now, crank up the music and let's celebrate!

P.S. Want to dive deeper into specific generations? Craving stories of individuals who shatter stereotypes? Stay tuned, because we're about to embark on a global dance party where everyone's invited, labels are left at the door, and the only requirement is an open mind and a willingness to groove!

Communication across the generations: Effective strategies for bridging the gap

Hold onto your smartphones and dust off your vinyl records, folks, because we're about to embark on a communication adventure! Today's mission: bridging the generation gap, one meme at a time! Imagine Baby Boomers swapping stories with Gen Z over TikTok trends, and Silent Generation wisdom mingling with Gen Alpha's VR dreams. Buckle up, time travelers, because effective communication across generations is the coolest superpower you can wield!

Think of generations like a diverse symphony: Boomers are the booming horns, Millennials the soulful strings, Gen Z the funky beats, and Alpha the experimental synths. Each brings a unique melody, but understanding their language is key to composing a harmonious future.

Here are some strategies to rock that intergenerational communication:

- **Ditch the jargon**: Leave the technical terms and emoji slang at the door. Speak plain English, peppered with a dash of curiosity about their vocabulary. Ask what "lit" means to grandma, and maybe she'll teach you a cool slang term from the roaring twenties.
- **Embrace active listening**: Put down your phone, make eye contact, and really hear what's being said. You might be surprised by the wisdom a Gen Z activist can share, or the hilarious stories a Silent Generation veteran has tucked away.
- **Seek common ground**: Everyone loves a good story, a delicious meal, or a shared laugh. Find that common thread – maybe it's music, movies, or a passion for gardening. Remember, grandma's meatloaf might just be the bridge to understanding her generation's struggles.
- **Respect the tech gap**: Not everyone is a digital native. Be patient, offer guidance, and remember, a little tech magic can open doors to new worlds. Teach grandma how to video call her grandkids, and who knows, you might end up learning a killer recipe for digital cookies from Gen Alpha.

- **Celebrate differences**: Embrace the unique perspectives and experiences each generation brings. Learn from each other, laugh at each other's jokes (even the bad ones), and remember, diversity is the spice that makes life interesting.

But remember, folks: There's no one-size-fits-all approach. Communication is a two-way street, paved with patience, respect, and a healthy dose of humor. So, the next time you encounter someone from a different generation, don't build walls, build bridges!

P.S. Craving tips on navigating digital divides or deciphering generational humor? Stay tuned, because we're about to embark on a global communication workshop where laughter is the language, memes are the currency, and everyone's invited to share their unique voice!

Chapter 7: The Future Unfolds: Generational collaboration and shaping the world to come

Looking beyond the alphabet: Embracing a continuous cycle of learning and evolution

Hold onto your textbooks and dust off your curiosity hats, folks, because today we're ditching the alphabet soup of generations and diving into a smorgasbord of learning! Forget rigid labels and neat boxes – every human, regardless of their birth year, is a walking, talking encyclopedia waiting to be cracked open. Buckle up, time travelers, because the real journey is the endless cycle of learning and evolution, where every generation brings a new dish to the table!

Think of it like a cosmic library with no Dewey Decimal System. Boomers are the leather-bound classics, Millennials the self-help paperbacks, Gen Z the interactive e-books, and Alpha the AI-powered virtual reality narratives. Each format holds unique knowledge, waiting to be devoured and digested.

So, why ditch the alphabet soup and embrace the learning buffet?

Every generation has a story: We're all walking history books, shaped by our own experiences, triumphs, and blunders. From Boomers witnessing the moon landing to Gen

Z navigating climate change, each generation has a unique perspective to offer.

Wisdom comes in all ages: Don't underestimate the power of a young mind or the depth of an experienced soul. A Gen Alpha kid might teach you the intricacies of blockchain technology, while a Silent Generation veteran can share the resilience learned through hardship.

Learning is a lifelong adventure: Curiosity and the pursuit of knowledge aren't bound by age. Embrace the continuous cycle of learning, where every interaction, every conversation, every book, and every meme becomes a stepping stone on your personal growth journey.

Embrace the diversity of knowledge: Just like a delicious buffet, the world of learning offers a variety of flavors. Don't stick to the familiar comfort food of your own generation. Sample the spicy wisdom of your elders, the tech-infused insights of the younger ones, and savor the unique blend of perspectives that every individual brings.

Challenge your own biases: We all have them, but that doesn't mean we can't work on them. Be open to new ideas, even if they differ from your own. Remember, learning isn't just about acquiring knowledge, it's about expanding your understanding of the world and yourself.

So, the next time you encounter someone from a different generation, don't assume you know everything they have to offer. Instead, approach them with an open mind and a curious heart. Ask questions, listen actively, and be ready to be surprised by the depth and richness of their knowledge.

Remember, folks, the learning buffet is vast and ever-expanding. There's no expiration date on curiosity, and no generation holds a monopoly on wisdom. So, grab your plate, pile it high with diverse perspectives, and embark on a lifelong journey of learning and evolution!

P.S. Want to explore specific areas of knowledge across generations? Craving tips on overcoming ageism and embracing intergenerational learning? Stay tuned, because we're about to embark on a global learning adventure where every generation is a professor, every experience a lesson, and the only requirement is an insatiable appetite for knowledge and growth!

Bonus Chapter

Gen Alpha Slang: Deciphering the code of a new generation

Hold onto your wigs, folks, because we're about to dive into the wild world of Gen Alpha slang! These digital natives were practically born with a smartphone in their cribs, and their language is evolving faster than you can say "OK, Boomer." So, whether you're a curious Millennial, a baffled Gen Xer, or a Boomer trying to keep up with the grandkids, grab your decoder rings and let's decipher the future's lingo!

Here's a crash course in Gen Alpha's vocabulary:

- - **"Rizz"** (short for "charisma") - It's what makes you magnetic, the ability to charm a room with a single emoji. If someone calls you "rizz," you're basically a social media superstar.

- - **"Gyat"** (slang for "that's good") - When something's epic, awesome, or just plain fire, Gen Alpha will hit you with a "gyat." It's like a virtual high-five, but way cooler.

- **"No Cap"** (meaning "no lie") - Want to emphasize your honesty? Add a "no cap" to your sentence. It's like a truth serum, but for digital conversations.

- **"Fanum"** (to pay a tax or fee) - Imagine paying your online dues with a single word. That's "fanum," a virtual currency of respect and acknowledgement.

- **"Doxxed"** (to reveal someone's personal information online) - A serious offense in the digital world, getting "doxxed" is like having your identity stolen, but with social media receipts. Not cool, Alphas, not cool.

But remember, folks, slang is like a living organism – it's constantly evolving and adapting. What's **"gyat"** today might be **"cringe"** tomorrow (and yes, **"cringe"** is still a thing in Alpha-land). So, how do you stay in the loop?

1. **Listen up**: Pay attention to how Gen Alpha talks in videos, social media posts, and even video games. You'll start to pick up on the trends.
2. **Ask the experts**: Got a Gen Alpha kid in your life? They're your personal slang dictionary. Just don't overuse their terms – nothing kills a trend faster than a parent trying to be "hip."
3. **Embrace the evolution**: Language is fluid, and that's a beautiful thing. Embrace the creativity and innovation of Gen Alpha's slang, and don't be afraid to experiment with your own language too!

So, the next time you hear a Gen Alpha say something that sounds like a foreign language, don't panic. Just grab your decoder ring, smile, and say "gyat." You got this, fellow language explorers!

Appendix

A detailed timeline of key events shaping each generation

Ah, generations! Those neatly packaged groups of people born within specific years, often defined by sweeping historical events and cultural trends. But hold on, time travelers, because these labels can be tricky. Let's ditch the dusty boxes and dive into a vibrant timeline, where each generation's story is woven with the threads of key events that shaped their lives. Buckle up, because we're about to embark on a journey through history, one impactful moment at a time!

The Silent Generation (1928-1945):

- Born into the shadow of the Great Depression, they learned resilience and resourcefulness early on.
- World War II defined their youth, forging a sense of unity and sacrifice.
- The post-war boom saw them rebuild nations, raise families, and lay the foundation for future generations.

Key events: The Dust Bowl, World War II, the rise of suburbs, the space race.

The Baby Boomers (1946-1964):

- Born amidst post-war optimism, they were the "free love" generation, challenging social norms and embracing individual expression.
- The Vietnam War and Civil Rights Movement ignited their activism, fighting for equality and social change.
- Technological advancements like the moon landing and the rise of the computer shaped their world.

Key events: The Vietnam War, the Civil Rights Movement, Woodstock, the moon landing, the rise of the personal computer.

Generation X (1965-1980):

- Witnessing the Cold War and economic instability, they developed a sense of cynicism and independence.
- Latchkey kids turned resourceful entrepreneurs, embracing DIY culture and side hustles.
- The rise of MTV and the personal computer gave them a tech-savvy edge.

Key events: The fall of the Berlin Wall, the AIDS crisis, the rise of cable television, the dot-com boom.

Millennials (1981-1996):

- Born into a world of technological advancement and globalization, they are digital natives and social media masters.
- 9/11 and the Great Recession shaped their awareness of global events and economic uncertainty.

- Champions of social justice and environmentalism, they are redefining success and work-life balance.

Key events: 9/11, the Great Recession, the rise of social media, the Black Lives Matter movement.

Generation Z (1997-2012):

- Growing up with smartphones and the internet, they are the VR-wielding, meme-speaking masters of the digital age.
- Climate change and political polarization are shaping their worldview, driving them towards activism and social responsibility.
- Entrepreneurs and side hustlers, they are redefining the future of work and creativity.

Key events: The rise of social media, climate change protests, the COVID-19 pandemic, the metaverse.

But remember, folks, these are just broad strokes on a vibrant canvas. Each generation is a kaleidoscope of experiences, personalities, and perspectives. The key is to understand that these timelines are not rigid boxes, but interconnected threads in the grand tapestry of human history.

So, the next time you encounter someone from a different generation, remember: their story is shaped by the events that came before yours. Ask questions, listen deeply, and celebrate the unique tapestry of experiences that each generation brings to the table. Together, we can weave a future rich with understanding, empathy, and a shared appreciation for the remarkable journey of humankind.

P.S. Want to delve deeper into specific generations? Craving a closer look at the cultural trends, music, and fashion that shaped them? Stay tuned, because we're about to embark on a time-traveling adventure where each generation is a vibrant destination, and every event is a portal to understanding the world we live in today!

Resources for further exploration and understanding

Hold onto your curiosity hats, fellow time travelers, because our journey through generations isn't over yet! We've cracked the code on historical events, unpacked slang secrets, and celebrated the individuality within each age group. But the rabbit hole of generational understanding goes much deeper, and we're about to equip you with the tools to keep exploring!

Ready to become a generational whisperer? Check out these resources:

Books:

- **"Generations: The History of America's Second Family"** by William Strauss and Neil Howe: This classic dives deep into the cyclical nature of generations, using history to predict future trends.

- **"The Silent Generation: Children of the Depression"** by Judith S. Wallerstein: A fascinating look at the generation shaped by hardship and resilience.
- **"Bowling Alone: The Decline of American Community"** by Robert D. Putnam: Explores the changing social fabric across generations, examining the decline of community involvement.
- **"The Defining Decade: Why Your Teens Are the Key to Our Future"** by Meg Jay: A Millennial psychologist gives advice on navigating your twenties and setting yourself up for success.
- **"I Do Things Better than You: A Guide to the Gen Z Mind"** by Joel Clark: Dive into the digital native world of Generation Z, understanding their motivations, communication styles, and values.

Documentaries:

- **"The Generational Divide"** (PBS): This series explores the unique characteristics and challenges of different generations.
- **"American Experience: Boomerang"** (PBS): A look at the Baby Boomer generation and their lasting impact on AmerThe Generational Divideican culture.
- **"Gen Z: Unfiltered"** (National Geographic): Get an up-close look at the lives and aspirations of Generation Z from around the world.
- **"The Millennials: Are They Worth It?"** (BBC): Explore the myths and realities surrounding the Millennial generation.

- **"Generation Silent: From the Dust Bowl to D-Day"** (PBS): A moving tribute to the Silent Generation and their contributions to American history.

Websites and Podcasts:

- **Pew Research Center**: A wealth of data and research on generations, demographics, and social trends.
- **Generations United**: A non-profit organization promoting intergenerational understanding and collaboration.
- **"Generational Harmony" podcast**: Host Jennifer Miller interviews experts on different generations and how to bridge the gaps.
- **"GenForward" podcast**: This NPR podcast explores the lives and experiences of Millennials and Generation Z.
- **"The Generation Project" podcast**: Interviews with people from different generations, sharing their stories and perspectives.

Don't forget: Engage with people from different generations! Strike up conversations with your grandparents, ask your teenage neighbor about their favorite memes, and listen to the stories of the veterans at your local park. Every interaction is a chance to learn, grow, and build bridges across the generational divide.

Remember, folks, understanding generations is not about putting people in boxes, it's about appreciating the unique tapestry of experiences and perspectives that each age group brings to the table. With the right resources and a curious mind, you can become a master navigator of the generational landscape, building bridges of understanding and celebrating the richness of human experience across the ages.

Now, go forth and explore! The future of intergenerational harmony awaits!

www.ingramcontent.com/pod-product-compliance
Lightning Source LLC
Chambersburg PA
CBHW071108260726
48661CB00006B/2541